# Persian Illustrated Manuscripts

# Persian Illustrated Manuscripts

G. M. MEREDITH-OWENS

PUBLISHED BY
THE TRUSTEES OF THE BRITISH MUSEUM
1973

First published 1965
Reprinted 1973

SBN 7141 0631 3

PRINTED IN GREAT BRITAIN
AT THE UNIVERSITY PRESS, OXFORD
BY VIVIAN RIDLER
PRINTER TO THE UNIVERSITY

# Contents


| | | |
|---|---|---|
| 1 | Introduction: Persian artistic conventions | page 7 |
| 2 | Persian literature and miniature painting | 8 |
| 3 | Persian illustrated manuscripts in the British Museum | 13 |
| 4 | Notes | 28 |
| 5 | Dates and dynasties in Persian history since the beginning of the Christian Era | 29 |
| 6 | Suggested reading | 30 |
| 7 | Index | 31 |

# Glossary

DĪNĀR — A gold coin worth about ten shillings.

DĪVĀN — A collection of poems by one author.

GHAZAL — An ode of not fewer than four and not more than fifteen couplets. The usual number is from five to ten. The first two hemistichs rhyme together while the others all have a single rhyme. Each couplet is complete in itself but the same idea runs through the poem—usually mystical love, but there are often allusions to the beauties of springtime, praise of wine and the unreliability of fortune.

IMĀM — According to the Shī'ah, one of the twelve successors of the Prophet in the line of 'Alī. The last of the twelve, the Hidden Imām, is expected to return. To the Sunnīs (the other great division of the Muslim world) the word Imām usually signifies a leader of any system of theology or law but in most cases it means the person who presides over the public prayers in the mosque.

QAṢĪDEH — Literally 'purpose-poem', usually written in honour of a rich patron whose name is introduced towards the end, or perhaps to commemorate some event such as the building of a palace or a disaster like an earthquake. The whole poem, which is much longer than a ghazal, is in a single rhyme. This form is much favoured by court poets and has no real counterpart in Western literature.

MAS̱NAVĪ — A type of verse-form, in rhyming couplets throughout, used for epics and various poems of didactic or mystical content.

PAHLAVI — The language of Persia, sometimes called Middle Persian, which developed after Avestan and Old Persian. After the Arab Conquest it merged into New Persian. It was written in a very ambiguous script derived from the Aramaic alphabet. The main difference between Middle and New Persian lies in the enormous Arabic element which has enriched the vocabulary in the last thousand years.

SIMURGH — A fabulous bird of Persian legend.

I. RAUẒAT UL-ANVĀR. Add. 18113, f. 85b. Sulṭān Malikshāh and the old woman. Timurid (Shiraz style).

II. SHAHANSHĀHNĀMEH. Or. 2780, f. 44b. The Mongols leaving the valley in which they had sought refuge from their enemies. Timurid (Shiraz style).

# 1 Introduction:
# Persian artistic conventions

It is impossible to give more than a brief survey of the art of Persian book illustration in these few pages owing to the large amount of material. We have therefore confined our remarks to the collection in the Department of Oriental Printed Books and Manuscripts of the British Museum.

To appreciate the art and skill of the Persian miniaturist, the beholder must accept implicitly the bonds of an entirely new set of conventions.[1] The figures are idealized symbols and realism was not a strong point. Rarely do we find a true portrait and perspective is non-existent but in time we do not miss its absence. In short, the artist's whole aim was to delight the eye of his patron, and the miniatures are no more than a specialized type of design but with an unsurpassed view for colour, dream-like in its beauty, meticulous in technique, with a good taste which holds its own until the advent of Western ideas. A nation of artists, in more than two thousand years of recorded history, the Persians were incapable of producing an unseemly form—even in the works of inferior craftsmen there is still a moderation and an innate feeling for what is correct.

While the orthodox Islamic dislike of the representation of living things was a barrier to the development of painting on a large scale, by keeping it well within the limits of book illustration, an advanced state of technical perfection was attained. This factor contributed much to the evolution of calligraphy and the arabesques found, not only as decorative motifs in manuscripts, but also in architecture. A similar formalism is to be seen in Persian poetry. The effect is the same—the workmanship is highly polished and refined, perfect in its own way, but following certain prescribed rules and traditions which are rigidly observed. These, to our mind, tend to obscure the poet's vision.

The range of illustrated manuscripts is somewhat restricted. Religious works are of course not illustrated except those of a more popular character like the exploits of 'Alī, the first Imām of the Shī'ah. Scientific works and medical treatises have few illustrations, and these are more in the nature of diagrams than miniatures. For the most part, illustration is found only in works of a 'fictional' character—the poetical romances, collections of poems (*dīvāns*) and poetical anthologies. Some chronicles written in rhymed prose or verse to glorify a reign or a dynasty also contain illustrations. The royal feats of arms are described in a magniloquent style which reflects that of the ancient epics. In addition to these illustrated works, there are the albums (*muraqqa'*) which are in a separate category as they contain little or no explanatory text. The result of this limited scope is that the same type of picture, with slight variations, is repeated over and over again, and remains virtually unchanged over the centuries.

# 2 Persian literature and miniature painting

The greater part of Persian illustrated manuscripts consists of poetical romances. To understand the immense popularity of these, we must turn to the literary background. After the Arab Conquest in the 7th century A.D., the national Pahlavi literature perished but the memory of the ancient kings and heroes never faded. The literary rebirth of the Persian nation begins when independent dynasties of Iranian stock arose in the most outlying Eastern provinces of the Caliphate. Some few quotations from romantic epics are preserved in the older anthologies but the greatest epic poem of Persia, the *Shāhnāmeh* (the Book of Kings) was begun by Daqīqī who was murdered by his favourite slave in A.D. 980. A far greater poet, Firdausī, completed the task in 60,000 verses in about A.D. 1010 and dedicated the completed work to his patron, Sultan Maḥmūd of Ghazneh—a fanatic who mistrusted Firdausī's religious views. Finding that his masterpiece had received a miserly reward, Firdausī fled to Ṭabaristān where he wrote a virulent satire against Maḥmūd in which he stigmatised the Sultan for his descent from Turkish slaves. For some time after this Firdausī lived in exile but returned to die at his birthplace, Ṭūs in Khurāsān, near the modern city of Meshed. The story goes that Maḥmūd sent a belated present of 60,000 dīnārs' worth of indigo—a rare and valuable gift at that time. As the camel which bore the load passed through the city gate, the funeral cortège of the poet was already leaving by another gate. The indigo was offered to Firdausī's only child, a daughter, but she proudly refused it and so, on the orders of the Sultan, the proceeds were used to build a rest-house.

The *Shāhnāmeh*, an epic in rhyming couplets, tells the story of the Persian kings from Gayūmarṣ who taught mankind the arts of civilization to the conquest of Iran by the Arabs whom Firdausī's Persians deride for their extreme simplicity of life. The *Shāhnāmeh* has become a source of national pride and even today on the Tehran Radio, extracts are recited daily to the roll of kettle-drums.

A new and more complex kind of verse is used by the next great writer of epic poems, Niẓāmī of Ganjeh (now Kirovabad in the Azerbaijan SSR). The diction becomes mannered in contrast with the simple couplets of Firdausī—each verse is overloaded with jewels—puns, subtle allusions and striking metaphors; consequently any version in another language needs copious notes. A similar artificial style was introduced into Persian prose some years previously, with assonance and parallelism very like that which became popular in England with the publication of Lyly's *Euphues* in 1579. After this date Persian epic poetry is modelled to a large extent on Niẓāmī's subtleties which, to our mind, detract from the vivid action and word-pictures of the poems.

Niẓāmī served some of the minor Seljuk Turkish rulers of his time and died in 1209.[2] He has left us a group of five poems, called the *Khamseh* or Quintet. The first of these is the *Makhzan ul-asrār* (Treasure-house of Secrets) and is a mystical epic divided into ten chapters, each containing illustrative anecdotes. This was Niẓāmī's first and last attempt at writing such a work. For his next poem he took as a theme the romantic story of the Sassanian King of Persia, Khusrau Parvīz (590–627) and the beauteous Armenian princess Shīrīn. An element of pathos, perhaps rather too exaggerated for our taste, permeates the poem. The third romantic epic of the group is *Lailā u Majnūn*, the tragic love of the Arab poet Qais for Lailā, a Bedouin maiden, daughter of a powerful Shaikh—a never-failing source of inspiration to the poets who came after Niẓāmī. The medieval Alexander Romance forms the subject of the fourth poem, the *Iskandarnāmeh*. It is divided into two parts, called *Iqbālnāmeh* and *Sharafnameh*. According to legend, Iskander was the son of the Persian king Dārāb by the daughter of Failaqūs (Philip of Macedon). She was banished by her husband owing to a quarrel, and returned to her father where she gave birth to Iskandar. This made him heir to the Persian throne, and it became a pretext for his attack on his younger half-brother Dārā (Darius III, Codomannus). After subduing the Persians, and all the other nations of the world, Iskandar went on his travels in quest of the Fountain of Life. An important role is played in this poem by Aristotle (Arisṭū) who acted as counsellor to Alexander. Lastly comes the *Haft paikar* (Seven Images) which, in the opinion of many scholars, is the finest poem of the five. It tells of another Sassanian monarch, Bahrām Gūr (420–38) who, in his youth, discovered seven portraits of lovely women in the Palace of Khavarnaq. Each represented a princess from a particular country—from India, China, Khvārazm,[3] Russia, Persia, Byzantium and Morocco. When Bahrām became king, he made all of them his brides, building a separate pavilion for each in the colour most appropriate to the place from which the princess came. On seven successive days he visited them and was regaled with a story by each of them somewhat in the manner of Shahrāzād and the Caliph in the *Arabian Nights*.

In his classic of Persian travel *A year among the Persians*, Browne says, 'The most striking feature of the Persians as a nation is their passion for metaphysical speculation'. Living in a land fruitful in religious ideas where life in this world has little to offer to the majority of its inhabitants, they have been constantly trying to solve the riddle of existence. Many Muslims, notably among the highly intellectual Persians, faced with the uncompromising dogma of Islam, looked for something more deeply satisfying to their souls. They found this in the Ṣūfī mysticism which had grown up among certain ascetics, at first largely of Arab stock, in the 9th and 10th centuries. It was once thought to have originated in the Neoplatonic philosophy but recent research has emphasized that there are esoteric elements inherent in the Koran itself.

The basic theme of Sufism is that the soul was exiled from God, its Beloved, and it longs to return and be absorbed in Him, as in the beautiful image of the reed which bewails its separation from the reed-bed.[4] To achieve permanent reunion, it is necessary to remove the barrier by annihilation of the flesh. This could be brought about by becoming a traveller (*sālik*) along a certain path under the guidance of a spiritual leader (*pīr*). An ecstasy like that produced by the whirling dance of the dervishes was merely a temporary reunion.

Sufism found a fertile soil in Persia and inspired most of the finest productions of Persian poetry. It gave rise to an elaborate imagery—Wine, the Tavern, Intoxication, the Ringlets and Cheek of the Beloved, all of which can be explained in a mystical sense. From this the transition to allegory was quite natural. Introduced by Sanā'ī (d.c. 1141) and developed by 'Aṭṭār, the mystical *maṣnavi* was perfected by Jalāl ud-Dīn Rūmī (d. 1273), the greatest name in Persian Sufism. He was born in Balkh and his family fled to Konya in Anatolia, probably because of the advancing Mongols. There he formed a circle of disciples which has survived in the Mevlevi order of Dervishes. The latter played a part of considerable importance in Turkish religious life and their leader, the Chelebi Efendi, invested every Sulṭān of Turkey with the sword of Osman as the insignia of his office.

Rūmī left a *dīvān* which he dedicated to his beloved friend, the wandering dervish Shams ud-Dīn of Tabriz, but his greatest work is the *Maṣnavī i ma'navī*. This poem, very ably translated by the late Professor Nicholson, is divided into six books and is a collection of stories in an everyday style, each of which contains an inner mystical meaning or inculcates some moral truth. Illustrated copies are rare. One such copy, dated about 1530, is in the British Museum collection; another, although of early date, contains miniatures in the traditional style but of modern workmanship.

A writer whose works the miniaturists of Iran are never tired of illustrating is Sa'dī of Shiraz (d. 1292), a very different type of person from Rūmī. Sa'dī took his pen-name from the grandson of the Atābeg of Fārs, Sa'd ibn Zangī. Orphaned at an early age, he studied at Baghdad and then performed the Mecca pilgrimage. He fought for the Faith and was taken prisoner by the Crusaders from whose hands he was delivered by a prominent citizen of Aleppo. The cost of his emancipation was an unhappy marriage with a veritable Xanthippe who made his life a misery. A much-travelled man, the counsel which he seeks to give in his anecdotes is very much of this world. The best-known work of Sa'dī is the *Gulistān*, a collection of anecdotes written in an elegant prose, each of which illustrates an ethical truth. Although comparatively short, this work is more celebrated than Sa'dī's *Būstān* which is a poem on a similar subject.

Amīr Khusrau of Delhi (d. 1325) was a prolific poet whose work, although written for the Turkish kings of Delhi, achieved great popularity in Persia as the number of illustrated copies attest. In addition to six *dīvāns*, Amīr Khusrau wrote historical poems to commemorate some event in the careers of his patrons and also five epics, choosing as subjects the romantic themes which Niẓāmī had treated with such skill. Amīr Khusrau is credited with the first verses written in Hindi but these are of very dubious authenticity. For all their grace and versatility, those Indian poets who come after the 'Parrot of India' (as he is called), have a somewhat exotic flavour for those more attuned to the writers of the Persian homeland.

Two illustrated copies still exist of the epics of Khvājū Kirmānī (d.c. 1352) who also followed the fashion inaugurated by Niẓāmī in writing a *Khamseh*. One of these is in the British Museum collection with three poems; the other is in Paris. The first poem of the five is the romance of Humāy and Humāyūn; the second, entitled *Naurūz u Gul*, is a similar love story of a prince of Khurāsān and a princess of Rūm (Asia Minor). With the others of the group—the *Kamāl-nāmeh*, *Rauẓat ul-anvār* and *Mafātīḥ ul-qulūb*, Khvājū turned to the Ṣūfī mysticism.

Apart from 'Umar Khayyām, more famous in his own country as a mathematician and astronomer, Ḥāfiẓ (d. 1389) is the Persian poet best known to Western readers, owing to the numerous excellent translations available. From the time of Sir William Jones (d. 1794), Ḥāfiẓ has been very fortunate in his translators. The edition of Professor Arberry containing fifty poems with translations, explanatory notes and some of his own versions, and those of Avery and Stubbs, published in the *Wisdom of the East* series, are particularly to be recommended. Several copies of the *Dīvān* of Ḥāfiẓ in the British Museum are illustrated. The miniatures are mostly of Indian origin, however, showing scenes of drinking parties, illustrating the many allusions to wine—the metaphysical Wine of Unreason.

Some poetical anthologies are occasionally illustrated. Add. 16561 is a fine example. This manuscript, dated 1468, was copied at Shīrvān in what is now Soviet Azerbaijan. Most of the miniatures refer to isolated lines in the *ghazals* like those in the Ḥāfiẓ manuscripts.

Jāmī (d. 1492), the last great classical poet of Iran, excelled in all branches of poetry. There are many copies of his collection of seven epics, the *Haft aurang*, in the British Museum. This work, the title of which means 'Seven Thrones', is called after a group of seven stars. The earliest of the seven, the didactic poem *Silsilat uẕ-ẕahab*, was completed before 1472. Then follows the romance of Salāmān and Absāl, a philosophical allegory translated by Fitzgerald in 1856, the *Tuḥfat ul-aḥrār* and *Subḥat ul-abrār*, both didactic, and the *Yūsuf u Zulaikhā* which gives the Eastern version of Yūsuf (Joseph), the 'Moon of Canaan', and Potiphar's wife as told in Surah XII of the Koran. This is by far the most popular work of Jāmī in the field of romance. The sixth poem is the story of Lailā and Majnūn which had already been treated with such distinction by Niẓāmī and Amīr Khusrau. The seventh, the *Khiradnāmeh i Iskandarī*, the 'Book of the Wisdom of Alexander', differs from the earlier poems on the Alexander theme in that it is not purely narrative.

Other romantic epics were illustrated from time to time but none as lavishly or as frequently as the foregoing. Niẓāmī, owing to his great popularity, is perhaps the most favoured author.

Illustrated chronicles are to be found in the British Museum of the campaigns of Tīmūr and the exploits of Shāh Ismā'īl, the founder of the Safavid dynasty, but there is nothing to compare in age and interest with the works of the historians of the Mongol Īlkhānī period in the Bibliothèque Nationale at Paris and in other collections. The technique of illustrating treatises on natural history is virtually confined to the '*Ajā'ib ul-makhlūqāt* (Wonders of Creation) by Qazvīnī, an author who flourished in the second half of the 13th century.

Miniatures occur in a copy, dated 1439–40, of the large collection of anecdotes by 'Aufī (d. c. 1230) entitled *Javāmi' ul-ḥikāyāt va lavāmi' ur-rivāyāt*, and in the *Miftāḥ ul-fuẓalā*, a very interesting illustrated dictionary of the rare words used by the older poets. With regard to the albums, one assembled towards the end of the 19th century contains good portraits of one of the rulers of the Zand dynasty and of the Qājārs, a family of Turkoman stock who supplanted them.

# 3 Persian illustrated manuscripts in the British Museum

In the British Museum there are nearly three hundred illustrated Persian manuscripts which include examples from the best periods of Persian and Indian painting. The earliest of these is the famous collection of *maṣnavī* poems by Khvājū Kirmānī. This manuscript (Add. 18113) contains three of the poems—the romantic epic of the love of Prince Humāy, the son of Shāh Hūshang, and Humāyūn, the daughter of the Emperor of China, the *Kamālnāmeh*, a mystical work, and the *Rauẓat ul-anvār* (Garden of Lights) which is an imitation of the *Makhzan ul-asrār* of Niẓāmī. The manuscript was copied at Baghdad in 1396 by the famous calligrapher Mīr 'Alī ibn Ilyās i Tabrīzī. Two of the miniatures are signed by the painter Junaid who may have painted all of them. This collection of poems is one of the first masterpieces of the Timurid period and in it is seen the genesis of the finer works which were yet to come. The illustration (Pl. I) is taken from the thirteenth *Maqāleh* (on kings being counselled to exercise justice) of the *Rauẓat ul-anvār*. It shows the old woman who sought redress for her wrongs from the Seljuk Sulṭān Malikshāh (1072–92). The elongated figures are typical of this period. This theme of an old woman approaching a monarch for justice is plainly derived from the much-illustrated scene in the *Makhzan ul-asrār* of Niẓāmī where the king is another Seljuk ruler, Sanjar (1117–1157). The braided pigtail appears in most of the other miniatures in this manuscript where women are shown. The story is that Malikshāh ibn Alp Arslān went forth from Isfahan on a hunting expedition. On the bank of the Zāyandeh-rūd river which passes through Isfahan, he was about to alight and change horses when an old woman darted out and seized his bridle. She reproached the Sulṭān eloquently for his selfishness. All he cared about was hunting while his subjects suffered great privations owing to his misrule. Malikshāh questioned her. She told him that she was a widow with four orphaned children. Their only sustenance was the milk of a cow which had been callously pursued by the king's retinue. These did not care what they did as the Sulṭān was remote and detached, knowing nothing of the misdeeds of his courtiers. She said 'You are half-drunk with the Wine of Carelessness and you have no knowledge of what is going on'. Malikshāh was greatly affected by the story and at once granted redress. The manuscript was formerly in the library of Abū'l-Fatḥ Bahrām, a Safavid prince and bibliophile who died in 1549.

The next Persian manuscript in point of date (Or. 2780) is a collection of epics copied by Muḥammad ibn Sa'īd Abdullāh in 1397–8, of which a p s to be seen in the Chester Beatty collection at Dublin. One of the poems in the manuscript was finished by the help of 'the most gracious King'—probably Aḥmad i Jalā'ir, who belonged to a dynasty which grew up in the ruins of the Mongol (Īlkhānī) Empire. It contains four epic poems entitled *Garshāspnāmeh*, *Shahanshāhnāmeh*, *Bahmannāmeh* and *Kūshnāmeh*, all of which deal with the deeds of legendary heroes except for the *Shahanshāhnāmeh*. This is a poem by Aḥmad i Tabrīzī on the history of the Mongol conqueror Chingiz Khān and his successors to the year 1337–8. In this poem, written by order of the Īlkhān Abū Sa'īd (d. 1335), the author traces the genealogy of the Mongols to Japheth the son of Noah. The Mongols at an early stage of their history were forced to yield to the Tartars who lived in the region of the Buir Nor. Following a defeat in 1161 at the hands of the Tartars allied with the Chinese, the two survivors of the race of Mongol Khān, named Qiyān[5] and Negüs, sought refuge with their wives in the valley of Ergene Kun. In this retreat, hemmed in by precipitous mountains, they remained for four hundred years, engaged in smelting iron from the ore which abounded in the district. The memory of this event was kept green by a ceremony performed every New Year's eve in the presence of the Mongol Khāns in which blacksmiths beat out the hot iron. When they emerged from their mountain fastness on to the plain, they went on from success to success until their armies overran the entire Orient and part of Eastern Europe. The illustration from this manuscript (Pl. II) is taken from the *Shahanshāhnāmeh* and shows the Mongols coming out from a mountain defile with all their pack-animals, oxen and other possessions. The chieftain who led them, Börte-chinua, wears a distinctive headdress but only his head and shoulders are visible in the picture.

The exquisite little manuscript Add. 27261 is a 'pocket-library' written for a grandson of Tīmūr, Jalāl ud-Dīn Iskandar ibn 'Umar Shaikh who ruled over Southern Persia. It was copied in 1410–11 by Muḥammad al-Ḥalvā'ī and Nāṣir ul-Kātib. Among the contents are the *Khamseh* of Niẓāmī, episodes from the *Shāhnāmeh* of Firdausī, various *qaṣīdehs* and *ghazals*, a manual of astronomy and other tracts. Several works, including the *Manṭiq uṭ-ṭair* of 'Aṭṭār, are in the margin. The illustration (Pl. III) shows a miracle of 'Alī as told in a *qaṣīdeh* by Futūḥī, a poet of the Seljuk period. On his way to Syria, 'Alī halted by a Christian monastery and saw a beautiful rose-cheeked lad who enquired where he was going. 'Alī explained that he was travelling from Medinah to Damascus. The

Christian, hearing this, was filled with love for Islam and praised the saintliness of 'Alī whom he did not recognize. He thought that 'Alī was Moses who had come once more to perform some miracle or Jesus who had come to rejoice mankind. 'Alī denied that he was one of the Prophets and a discussion as to his identity ensued. At length 'Alī said 'They call me Ḥaidar' (the lion),[6] and he recited a Koranic text whereupon the Christian monk jumped over the monastery wall 'like a pigeon with wings seared by the sun', uttering a piercing cry 'Thou art God'. He would have fallen to his death but 'Alī sent an angel to support him so that he landed safely. The monks, seeing the miracle, became Muslims at once and 'Alī went on his way. 'Alī, holding a rosary, is seated by the stream. The head of his famous mule Duldul is visible on the extreme left. The falling of the monk (here with a grey beard!) is depicted very clearly and naturally, by the way his none-too-monkish garments hang downwards. Two men who also do not wear the dress of Christian monks watch from inside the lattice window. The green tiles around the dome and elsewhere show an elaborate tracery which is slightly raised in some places. The bell with a double clapper is interesting.

One of the finest and most famous works of art of the Timurid period is another small manuscript (Add. 25900) which is dated 1442. Of the nineteeen miniatures only the one which has been selected (Pl. IV) is contemporary with the manuscript. Another bears an inscription that it was painted in 1493. The importance of this manuscript lies in the fact that it contains three miniatures signed by the celebrated painter Bihzād. It is a copy of the *Khamseh* of Niẓāmī and the illustration shows Shīrīn looking at the portrait of Khusrau Parvīz, a Sassanian ruler of Persia, whose friend Shāhpūr, a skilful painter, told him about the niece of Mihīn Bānū, the Queen of Armenia. This lovely maiden Shīrīn engaged in hunting expeditions with three hundred maidens to attend her. Some time previously Khusrau had been informed in a dream by his grandsire Nūshīrvān the Just[7] that he would meet a beautiful girl of this name, so he sent his friend Shāhpūr to Armenia to negotiate a royal marriage. While staying at a monastery, Shāhpūr heard that Shīrīn with her hunting-train was expected to pass by. He painted a portrait of Khusrau which he hung on a tree in a place where Shīrīn could not fail to see it. Shīrīn was greatly impressed by the picture but her attendants told her that it was a work of darkness. They tore up the picture but Shāhpūr, who was hiding nearby, painted another portrait. The same thing occurred once more but the third portrait survived the suspicion of the girls. Shāhpūr, in the dress of a Christian priest, came out of his hiding place, told Shīrīn how his illustrious master had fallen in love with her and he gave Shīrīn a ring from Khusrau as a token of love. She left her aunt and made for the Persian capital, Ctesiphon. On the way Khusrau who had been exiled owing to a quarrel with his father engineered by intriguing courtiers, saw Shīrīn bathing in a pool. In the illustration the faces on the rocks are a device frequently introduced by painters of the Timurid period.

A copy of the *Javāmi' ul-ḥikāyāt* (Or. 11676), dated 1439–40, is virtually unknown outside the British Museum, although it contains some interesting miniatures in a provincial version of the Shiraz style in a fine state of preservation. Towards the middle of the 16th century, further miniatures, in the Bukhara style, were added and later still, Indian artists filled blank spaces in the manuscript with pictures and decorative motifs. The *Javāmi' ul-ḥikāyāt va lavāmi' ur-rivāyāt* is a collection of 2,113 anecdotes, some of great historical value, compiled by Sadīd ud-Dīn Muḥammad 'Aufī, a Persian man of letters, better known for his *Lubāb ul-albāb* which is the earliest surviving biography of Persian poets. 'Aufī settled in India at the court of the ruler of Sind, but later transferred his allegiance to Iletmish, one of the Turkish 'Slave-Kings' of Delhi. His death took place about 1230.

Plate IX depicts an incident when the Abbasid Caliphs seized power from the Umayyad Dynasty in 749–50. During the reign of Marwān II, the last of the Umayyad Caliphs, there was a serious insurrection in the eastern provinces of the Arab Empire. All who were discontented with the Umayyad régime made common cause under the black banner of Abū Muslim, a Persian freedman of obscure origin who was the mainspring of the rebellion. Marwān seized Ibrāhīm, the caliph-designate of the rival Abbasid house and brought about his death in prison. His brothers, Abū'l-'Abbās, Abū Ja'far, 'Īsa and Mūsa, fled to Kūfah where they were hidden by Abū Salamah, the Vinegar-seller, behind a curtain in his house. He told them that he favoured their cause but advised them to remain in hiding until the moment was propitious. In the meantime Qaḥṭabah, one of the lieutenants of Abū Muslim, carried all before him in his campaign against the nearest Umayyad army led by Ibn Hubairah. Qaḥṭabah was drowned in the Euphrates but his two sons returned to Kūfah where they besought Abū Salamah to bring out the successor of Ibrāhīm and acclaim him as caliph. Abū Salamah demurred because he secretly hoped that the caliphate would go to the Shī'ah descendents of 'Alī rather than to the Abbasids from whom he kept the latest developments concealed. From their hiding-place the Abbasids sent a slave to investigate matters. By this means they heard of the arrival of the sons of Qaḥṭabah. They ordered the slave to go to Ḥamīd, the son of Qaḥṭabah, asking him to bring up his army without informing Abū Salamah so that they could emerge and seize the caliphate with the aid of their armed supporters. Ḥamīd was overjoyed and occupied the house of Abū

III. MISCELLANY. Add. 27261, f. 305b. A miracle performed by ʻAlī.
Timurid (Shiraz style).

IV. KHAMSEH. Add. 25900, f. 41a. Shīrīn sees the picture of Khusrau. Timurid (Later Herat style).

Salamah who was away at the time. Leaving some of his men on guard at the door of the underground chamber where the four Abbasids were concealed, he entered and greeted them. Ḥamīd hailed Abū'l-'Abbās as caliph because he fulfilled the conditions laid down by the murdered Ibrāhīm and made all present acknowledge him at the point of the sword. Then Ḥamīd brought Abū'l-'Abbās to the mosque and the new caliph[8] went up into the pulpit while his uncle 'Abdullāh stood a little lower. Abū'l-'Abbās delivered his inaugural *khuṭbah*[9] and all the congregation swore allegiance to him.

In the accounts of this event given by other authors, Abū Muslim was the first to greet Abu'l-'Abbās as caliph. He walked before the caliph who rode a piebald horse in procession to the mosque.

The other miniature from this manuscript shows the Abbasid Caliph al-Mahdī (775–85) being massaged by his slaves. The story tells how a mighty famine took place in his time which neither the caliph nor his officials could alleviate. He was accustomed to take his ease lying on a couch while a number of slaves massaged his hands and feet. One night he was unable to sleep and summoned one of his slaves. Al-Mahdī asked the slave to tell him what was in his mind. He replied that it was not fit for the Prince of the Believers to hear. The caliph persisted so the slave said 'There was a fertile land in India in which lived a lion. Other wild beasts living near came to see him and waxed fat upon the remains of his meals. Then a fox came and said, "You must be King and a King must take care of his subjects. I have a small cub and I want you to look after him and protect him from enemies while I go on a journey." The lion agreed to his request. Suddenly an eagle swooped from the sky and carried away the cub. When the fox returned, he came to the lion and asked about his offspring. He protested that the lion had promised to ensure the cub's safety. The lion said, "I was to answer for his safety on the land but I did not guarantee to protect him from the creatures of the air".' When al-Mahdī heard this, he burst into tears. Here we have the age-old device (which we find in many Oriental fables), of presenting distasteful political truths through the mouths of animals. In the picture the folds in the curtains are skilfully painted; likewise the floral designs on the tiles are picked out in gold. The men's faces with goatee beards and moustaches are typical of some versions of the Shiraz style.

Add. 6619 is a copy of the poetical romance *Mihr u Mushtarī*, dated 1472, with eight miniatures. The author, 'Aṣṣār of Tabriz, wrote this poem in 1376–7, and at one time it enjoyed great popularity. According to the preface, 'Aṣṣār had little success in writing eulogies to princes so that he gave up poetry but a friend persuaded him to try his hand at a *maṡnavī* poem. The result was this romance—'the story of a love which is free from every frailty and pure from every sensual lust between Mihr, the son of King Shāhpūr, and the comely lad, Mushtarī.' The latter was the son of the vizier to King Shāhpūr of Persia. Mushtarī was educated with the young prince Mihr and loved him as David loved Jonathan. The prince's envious tutor Bahrām intrigued with the king to separate the two friends so that Mihr was imprisoned in a castle by his angry father while Mushtarī was banished from Persia. At last Mihr escaped and, while searching for his friend, found himself at the court of King Kaivān of Khvārazm whose lovely daughter Nāhīd lost her heart to him. Mihr helped her father against Qarā Khān, the King of Samarkand, but he did not forget his friend Mushtarī. The latter had fallen into the hands of the evil Bahrām, and hearing of his plight, Mihr persuaded the King of Khvārazm to rescue him. The two friends were at last united and became reconciled to the old King of Persia before his death. Mihr reigned wisely, with Mushtarī acting as his vizier, but died soon after of a dangerous malady. Strange to say, Mushtarī died of the same disease, and the two friends were buried in one tomb. Shortly after, Nāhīd died of grief and left a son to succeed Mihr as King of Persia. In the illustration (Pl. X) Mihr is shown playing polo with Kaivān. This was a test of strength and agility, and was the sixth of eight trials held to prove whether the education of Mihr was equal to the king's conjectures respecting his noble birth. The poem says that Kaivān was so active that he carried away the orb of the sun from the sky—a play on the words *gūy* which means not only 'orb' but also 'ball', and *Mihr* which is the Persian name for the sun. The effort of the game is shown on the faces of the riders.

We come now to the first of the two illustrated *Shāhnāmeh* manuscripts described in this book. This is Add. 18188, a large and fine copy with seventy-two miniatures, transcribed in 1486 by Ghiyās̱ ud-Dīn ibn Bāyazīd i Ṣarrāf. Plate XI shows the episode when Bahman, on a mission from his father Isfandiyār, saw from the heights of a mountain their rival Rustam below. The latter had taken off his armour to rest while he roasted a wild ass for his meal. Rustam's horse Rakhsh was turned loose to browse on the rich grass by the stream. Bahman saw a golden opportunity of ridding himself and his father of a dangerous adversary. He determined to kill Rustam by rolling a flinty boulder on him. Rustam's brother, Zavāreh, who was with him, heard the rumble of the falling rock and warned Rustam. The latter waited calmly, wine-flagon in hand, until the stone was nearly on him. Then with a kick he sent it far away. Bahman decided then and there that such a man was too powerful to overcome in fair combat so he resolved to deal with him diplomatically. Thereupon he greeted Rustam courteously, and after the customary exchange of compliments, they sat down together to eat. Bahman was no less amazed at Rustam's skill as a trencherman than he was at his prodigious strength and vigour. The very realistic fire is noteworthy in this miniature, and the deep green vegetation is typical of the Turkman style.

Another manuscript (Or. 6810) containing miniatures by Bihzād is also a *Khamseh* of Niẓāmī. This copy is undated but on f. 214 a date corresponding to 1494 appears in an inscription. The names of the artists Mīrak, 'Abd ur-Razzāq, and Bihzād are inscribed singly or in pairs on nineteen of the twenty-two miniatures; but some of these are later attributions. The manuscript was at Agra in 1564–5 and came into the possession of the Mughal Emperors Jahāngīr and Shāh Jahān as attested by autograph notes concerning the miniatures. Of these, five may be by Bihzād's master, and fourteen are connected with Bihzād himself or his pupils. The name Qāsim 'Alī also appears but was evidently added later as Jahāngīr does not mention it. The miniature selected from this manuscript (Pl. V) is from the *Haft paikar* and is the story told in the Green Dome by the daughter of the King of the Fourth Clime. Bishr, a saintly man of Rūm, saw a beautiful maiden and his thoughts were turned to worldly matters. To remedy this, he went on a pilgrimage to Jerusalem, and on his return, he fell in with a man named Malīkhā who boasted of his knowledge and asked questions which were dangerously close to challenging God's decrees. After several days' journey the two of them reached a tree, the shade of which invited them to rest in the heat of the day. Beside it was a large earthen jar full of water let into the ground to refresh the weary traveller. An argument ensued as to how the jar got there. Bishr said that some kind person had placed it there for the use of travellers and it had been embedded in the ground to protect it from breakage. Eventually Malīkhā, who claimed that the jar was to attract thirsty animals to a snare, stepped into the jar to bathe. It was no jar but a deep well and so Malīkhā was drowned. Bishr broke a branch and fished out the body and gave his friend decent burial. He then took possession of his effects, including some gold coins, intending to take them to Malīkhā's friends. He reached a town, and after making enquiries, was directed to a house where a beautiful maiden lived who turned out to be the widow of Malīkhā. Later she married Bishr.

This is one of the tales of mystical meaning very frequently encountered in Persian literature. The beautiful maiden is the Beloved of the Ṣūfīs, whose beauty the soul has once beheld but from which it has since become separated, and to which it yearns to return. The two travellers are following the mystical path. The jar and the water represent the profundity of the Ṣūfī doctrine which appears simple on the surface but is really like a bottomless well, dangerous to the profane, and there is no use speculating as to its nature. The composition of the illustration shown is full of pathos—the deep *qanāt*,[10] the inert body, the desolate landscape and the autumnal tints of the leaves.

One of the most popular mystical allegories in Persian is the well-known *Manṭiq uṭ-ṭair* of Farīd ud-Dīn 'Aṭṭār, a talented and prolific poet who died in 1190.[11] It is an elaboration of a work by the famous philosopher al-Ghazzālī (d. 1111) in which the birds, led by the Hoopoe, set out to seek the Sīmurgh whom they had elected as their king. The journey of the birds represents the Ṣūfī Path. The birds make excuses and raise difficulties on their departure to which the Hoopoe replies, illustrating his discourse with numerous anecdotes. All but thirty of the birds perish on the way in the crossing of seven dangerous valleys—of Quest, Love, Knowledge, Self-sufficiency in God, Unification, Amazement at the loving proximity of God and Annihilation which indicate the various stages on the Path. The thirty (*sī-murgh* = thirty birds) who survive the arduous journey and reach the Sīmurgh, recognize themselves as being the Deity. They are then merged and finally absorbed in the divine Sīmurgh.

The plate (XII) shows the Peacock[12] introducing himself to the Hoopoe. With his gilded feathers 'like the colour of early spring' he displays himself proudly, saying 'Although I am the Gabriel among birds, my lot has been unhappy. I was friendly with the loathly Serpent but for this I fell from Paradise in ignominy. Since they banished me from there, ill-fortune has been, as it were, a fetter on my feet, but I have always hopes that someone will guide me out of this dark place to the Abode of Bliss. I am not that bird who will reach the King's door—it will be enough for me to reach the porter at the gate.' The sole desire of the Peacock was to return to the earthly Paradise.

The manuscript (Add. 7735), which has no colophon, dates from between 1490 and 1500 approximately. It has nine miniatures and belonged in the year 1705 to Allāh-verdī Khān, the *Beglerbegi* of Shīrvān.

Only one of the numerous Persian glossaries in the British Museum is illustrated. This is Or. 3299 entitled *Miftāḥ ul-fuẓalā* by Muḥammad ibn Dā'ūd ibn Muḥammad ibn Maḥmūd Shādīyābādī. The author lived in India during the second half of the 15th century. The Hindi equivalent has been given for many of the words. This adds to the value of the glossary which was compiled in 1468–9. The manuscript probably dates from the early 16th century, judging by the miniatures which resemble those of the Turkman style. In view of the colour scheme and various peculiarities of dress, it is very likely that this manuscript was illustrated by a Persian artist working in Western India. Plate XIII(a-b) illustrates the words *dastās* (a quern or hand-mill) and *darafsh* (a standard or pennant). The other miniature from this manuscript (Pl. XIII(c)) represents the word *nushreh* which is an amulet or talisman to avert evil from children, written with saffron on a red or yellow writing board. The scene, set in a Koran school, shows the old teacher with ferula seated upon a mat. A servant brings a gilt dish with brown top (probably containing saffron). The Arabic letters can be seen written on a writing-board held by two pupils. Another pupil sits by a lectern with an open Koran in the background. The text mentions that the amulet is given to boys after completing the reading of the Koran or one of its thirty portions.

There are several copies of the *'Ajā'ib ul-makhlūqāt* of Qazvīnī with illustrations. The finest and most recently acquired of these is Or. 12220, written by Shams ud-Dīn ibn Ghiyās̱ ud-Dīn al-Ḥāfiẓ al-Sharīf al-Kirmānī at Herat in 1503-4. It contains 443 miniatures, mostly quarter-size like those illustrated here. Plate XIV shows Iskandar (Alexander the Great) sailing the circumambient Ocean. The narrative, on the authority of al-Samarqandī, states that Iskandar sailed upon this sea for a whole year but did not reach the further shore—only the surface of the water was seen as far as the eye could stretch. Although some of his companions wished to return, others said 'Let us sail on for another month'. This they did and saw a vessel with men on it who spoke no known tongue. They exchanged one of their own men for a woman of these strange people and returned, following the route they had travelled. In the illustration, Iskandar looses an arrow and brings down a white bird. The boat is painted black (to indicate pitch?) and has a curved prow. As is usually the case, the silver of the sea has become badly oxydized.

The second miniature from this manuscript shows a giraffe. Qazvīnī states that it has a head like that of an ostrich, the teeth and horns of a cow and the skin of a leopard. It has legs like those of a camel but shorter at the front than at the back. He says that it is born of an Abyssinian she-camel and a wild ox or a male hyaena.

The more interesting of the two illustrated copies of the *Mas̱navī* of Jalāl ud-Dīn Rūmī (Add. 27263) with nineteen miniatures was probably copied and illuminated around 1530. Most of the miniatures have been retouched at a later date. Plate XV depicts the story of the Travellers and the Elephant in Book III. In India a wise man saw a party of his friends travelling along a road. They were in great distress through lack of food, but the sage warned them against eating the young elephant which they would encounter on the road, lest the mother elephant should attack them 'with fire and smoke issuing from her trunk'. They disregarded his advice, killed and roasted the elephant calf. During the night when they were all sleeping off a surfeit of roast meat, the mother appeared and sniffed at each man to see whether he smelt of roast elephant. All but one who had heeded the words of the sage smelt of this. Him she spared but tore all the others to pieces. Like the rest of the stories in the *Maṣnavī* this is a parable. The young elephants represent the righteous and innocent, the prophets and saints of this world, while the smell is that of greed and sin which cannot be concealed. The mother elephant symbolizes the inexorable Judgment which will overtake the wicked. In a version of this story by another author, the cow elephant takes the innocent man to a place of safety. In this spirited illustration, the elephant, which resembles those in medieval bestiaries, bears a saddlecloth of rose colour and pale green.

The next manuscript (Or. 2265) is one of the most sumptuous in the entire collection. It is a copy of the *Khamseh* of Niẓāmī, written for Shāh Ṭahmāsp between 1539 and 1543 by the famous calligrapher, Shāh Maḥmūd Nīshāpūrī, called 'Golden Pen'. It contains miniatures signed by the best artists of the age—Mīrzā 'Alī, Sulṭān Muḥammad, Mīr Sayyid 'Alī, Āqā Mīrak and Muẓaffar 'Alī. Three of the miniatures show signs of Western influence of which two, dated 1675, are signed by Muḥammad Zamān, an artist trained in Italy. In one of these (Pl. XVI), an illustration of Bahrām Gūr killing the dragon, the face of Bahrām is probably a portrait of the reigning Shāh, Sulaimān (1666–94). The story behind the other miniature selected for this book (Pl. VI) is of King Nūshīrvān who, while hunting, was separated from all his companions. Only his vizier remained with him. They passed by a ruined and deserted village where two owls (the symbol of desolation) were perching on a wall, calling to each another. The Vizier explained that there was a dispute between them about the size of the dowry of the daughter of one of the birds who had been given in marriage to the other. He wanted a ruined village or two thrown in. The other owl replied 'If this king reigns over us much longer, there will be ruins enough to spare for us all'. The king was greatly upset by this imputation of incapacity and injustice and was filled with remorse. He galloped back to his camp with such haste that the shoes of his horse melted away. At once Nūshīrvān took measures to make amends for his exactions and tyranny, and he is now called Nūshīrvān the Just.

The first of the historical chronicles to be described is Add. 7784, the *Shāhnāmeh i Ismā'īl* of Mīrzā Muḥammad Qāsim Junābādī who adopted the pen-name of Qāsimī. It is a history of Shāh Ismā'īl (1500–23), one of the greatest figures of his time who made the Shī'ah the state religion of Persia and founded the Safavid Dynasty. He traced his descent from a holy man who lived at Ardabīl in the 14th century. Shāh Ismā'īl wrote poems in Azeri Turkish which was his mother-tongue. In 1500, at the age of fourteen, Ismā'īl marched at the head of 7,000 men on Shīrvān where his ancester Shaikh Junaid had suffered martyrdom. The ruler of Shīrvān, Farrukh-yasār, encountered Ismā'īl and his

Turkoman Qızıl-bash followers in battle. The Shīrvān-shāh was taken prisoner and his head brought to Shāh Ismā'īl. All the fortresses of Shīrvān were reduced one by one including the fort of Baku. Ismā'īl carried his vengeance even to the point of exhuming the ancestors of Farrukh-yasār and burning their bones. The Shīrvān-shāh was only the first of Ismā'īl's adversaries. He overcame in succession Alvand Mīrzā, the ruler of Azerbaijan, Sulṭān Murād, ruler of Iraq and Fārs, Ḥusain Kiyā-i Chalavī, 'Atā' ud-dauleh Ẕū' l-Qadr Khān and the Uzbek Shaibānī Khān whose skull he made into a drinking vessel. In 1514 he fought the Ottoman Turks at Chāldirān but was defeated, largely owing to the power of the Turkish artillery.

The *Shāhnāmeh i Ismā'īl* is in the style and metre of the *Shāhnāmeh* of Firdausī. It was begun in the reign of Shāh Ismā'īl but was not completed until 1533. The British Museum manuscript is dated 1541, and contains thirteen miniatures which match the ancient heroic atmosphere of the poem, although in many respects they are realistic. Plate XVII shows Shāh Ismā'īl, riding a horse with gilded armour. He charges diagonally down the mountain-side in pursuit of the Shīrvān-shāh who is on the point of being captured. One man-at-arms bears a targe equipped with a spear; another blows an immensely long trumpet while a third beats a kettle-drum mounted on a camel's back. The golden sky contains wispy clouds fringed with an angry red.

Another scene from this manuscript (Pl. XVIII) shows Shāh Ismā'īl hunting various animals, including wild asses, bears and ibexes. While his retinue look on, the Shāh, mounted on his white horse, transfixes a lion with an arrow.

Hilālī, whose poems appear in the next manuscript, was of Turkish stock. He was the author of a *maṣnavī* called *Shāh u Gadā* 'The King and the Beggar', another entitled *Ṣifāt ul-'Āshiqīn* 'The Attributes of Lovers', and a number of *ghazals*. He was unlucky enough to fall foul of the fanatical Uzbek 'Ubaidullāh Khān who had him killed in 1528. The manuscript (Or. 4124) is a beautiful little work in perfect condition, typical of the period with fine illuminated head-piece and marginal decorations in gold. It was copied in 1550 by a famous calligrapher, Sulṭān Muḥammad Nūr, and the binding, in gold and black lacquer, bears the figures of animals with flying angels on the flap. In addition to the *Shāh u Gadā*, the manuscript contains the *Ṣifāt ul-'Āshiqīn*, a mystical work in which every section includes an appropriate anecdote. The plate (XIX) shows the story of Zulaikhā told in Chapter 20 (On the Unity of God). Finding herself growing old and losing her beauty, Zulaikhā kept an idol (golden in the miniature) hidden away which she secretly worshipped. All her thoughts were on love for Yūsuf but, since she obtained no response from the idol—'that idol has become a stone on the Road of my Desire', she decided to smash it with a hard stone. This she did and 'stopped the chinks in her faith with fragments of the idol'.

The story of Yūsuf and Zulaikhā appears with greater prominence in Or. 4535, a copy of Jāmī's famous romance, dated about 1550–60. Zulaikhā summoned the ladies of Egypt to a feast. They had criticized her unrequited love for Yūsuf 'that Hebrew slave' and she wished to confound them by letting them see him in person. The feast was arranged with all the luxury and elegance of the time. A feature of the entertainment was that oranges, said to be good for bile, were served, with knives. The ladies declared that they would not cut into their oranges until they had seen Yūsuf. The climax came and Yūsuf appeared in fine raiment. The ladies of Egypt were so struck by his beauty that they cut their fingers severely. They were forced to admit that Zulaikhā's passion for Yūsuf was completely justified. There came a cry from them 'He is no mortal man—like Adam he is not fashioned from water and clay but he is a celestial being from on high'. The ladies were so smitten with him that they then and there offered themselves to him. Yūsuf prayed to be sent to prison to escape from all the women who were pursuing him. His prayer was granted. Zulaikhā, ostensibly to clear her honour but really hoping to coerce him into accepting her advances, suggested to her husband that Yūsuf should be imprisoned. She told the gaoler, however, to treat him kindly and came secretly to gaze upon him. As in the Bible story, Yūsuf interpreted the dreams of his fellow-prisoners.

Plate VII shows the scene when Yūsuf (with halo) enters on the right. Zulaikhā, wearing a diadem, stands in the centre. On the other side, somewhat damaged, are servants bringing bowls of sherbet on a golden tray while in the subterranean kitchen a cook is stirring a pot with a ladle. Features of interest are the delicate plumed crests of the ladies, the gold decorated with pointillé work, and the blue and white porcelain of Chinese origin.

With Or. 1359 we come to a different type of illustration. The manuscript is the *Ẓafarnāmeh* of the court chronicler and stylist, Sharaf ud-Dīn 'Alī Yazdī. It is based upon the official histories of the reign of Tīmūr and was completed in 1424. This copy, which has a handsome gilt lacquer binding, was transcribed in 1552 by Murshid al-'Aṭṭār and Ḥasan al-Sharīf al-Kātib, and contains nineteen miniatures. Plate VIII shows the captured Ottoman Sulṭān, Bāyezīd I, 'the Thunderbolt', brought before Tīmūr. Between the two most powerful figures of the extreme East and West of the Muslim world a rivalry had arisen which had been exacerbated by each ruler harbouring the enemies of the other. Various Anatolian Turkish princelings dispossessed by Bāyezīd's efforts to become the overlord of Asia Minor, had sought refuge with Tīmūr. Bāyezīd, in turn, had given asylum to Sulṭān Aḥmad i Jalā'ir of

V. KHAMSEH. Or. 6810, f. 175a. A story from the Haft paikar. Bishr recovers the body of his friend Malīkhā from the well. Timurid (Later Herat style).

VI. KHAMSEH. Or. 2265, f. 15b. King Nūshīrvān and the owls. Safavid (Tabriz style).

Baghdad and the Turkoman chieftain Qarā Yūsuf, both of whom were wanted alive or dead by Tīmūr. In 1402 the Tartar hordes of Tīmūr, reinforced from his capital, Samarkand, moved towards Asia Minor. An embassy which came from Bāyezīd to negotiate with him had no result, so the Ottoman Turks began to make preparations. Bāyezīd was forced to abandon the siege of Constantinople and face this approaching menace on his Eastern frontier. Tīmūr's army advanced as far as Ankara which was at once invested. The defences of the city were just beginning to crumble when news was received by Tīmūr of the rapid advance of the Ottoman army from Sivas to raise the siege. The Ottoman Turks had made a forced march and water was scarce as the Tartars controlled the wells. They were thus in no position to face a powerful army led by the great captain of the age. The two armies clashed in a valley near Ankara. Despite the desperate bravery of the Janissaries and the Serbian cavalry led by Bāyezīd's brother-in-law Lazarović, the Ottomans were defeated. This was owing to the desertion of some of their Tartar auxiliaries and vassals whose sympathies were with Tīmūr. Bāyezīd was taken prisoner and brought before Tīmūr who treated him with great consideration until he attempted to escape. After this, he was chained at night, and travelled in a litter surrounded by a grille carried between two horses until his death in 1403. The Ottoman Turks did not recover from this disaster for some time, owing to the strife between the sons of Bāyezīd. Two features of interest in this illustration are the variety of plumed headdresses and the elaborate furnishings of the pavilion which contains a carpet with a striking red, pale blue and black design, and is provided with two openings at the top to admit light and air. Bāyezīd, who wears armour of reinforced leather or brown lacquered metal plates, is brought in with hands roped behind his back by two Tartars, one of whom wears the characteristic bonnet. There is a similar group of illustrations in another copy in the British Museum (Add. 7635, dated 1523). This is noteworthy for its pictures of an early cannon and a siege engine in action. One manuscript of the *Ẓafarnāmeh* at Princeton has several miniatures attributed to Bihzād.

The frequency of illustrated copies of the works of Sa'dī has already been mentioned. Perhaps the finest of these in the British Museum is Add. 24944 which was copied in 1566. The paintings and the illumination were completed two years later. This manuscript, which is of a large size, contains only two full-page miniatures. The others are considerably smaller. One of these (Pl. XX) illustrates an anecdote from the second chapter of the *Gulistān* which deals with the manners of dervishes. At one time Sa'dī was travelling to Arabia on the pilgrimage to Mecca. He was with a party of virtuous and spiritually-minded young men who were accustomed to chant sacred songs and recite mystical verses; but a devotee who was with them held a poor opinion of dervishes. When they reached a place where the Arab tribe of Hilāl lived, a black boy appeared and sang so sweetly that 'he stopped the birds in their flight through the air'. Sa'dī tells us that he saw the devotee's camel begin to prance so that it threw its rider and ran away into the desert. He said to the prostrate man 'O Shaikh, those strains made an impression on an animal, did they not move you?'

The other illustration from this manuscript is a lively scene (Pl. XXI) which forms a pair with a picture of the tomb of Sa'dī at Shiraz—a popular rendezvous. Many manuscripts of the works of Sa'dī which date from this period contain these two scenes. Near the tomb there is a subterranean pool which was once famous for its health-giving properties. The inhabitants of Shiraz used to bathe in it, particularly on the evening of the last Wednesday before the New Year Festival (*Naurūz*). The pool still contains a great number of fish which were formerly held sacred on account of their association with the poet's last resting place. In some of the other manuscripts with this scene, the fish are shown. It is not known which ruler is looking on but he is nearly always shown wearing garments of a Timurid type, and has rather Turkic features. He is sometimes accompanied by two young princes. Perhaps there was an early prototype, now lost, which was imitated by generations of artists. Here the king, with an aigrette in his cap, is wearing a pale green tunic and blue trousers. On the right are a heap of tambourines and a flute-player. Towels are hanging up to dry in the alcove behind the king. The artist has evidently great skill in depicting crowds, and many of the faces incline towards caricature.

Add. 7753, the *Qirān us-Sa'dain* of Amīr Khusrau, is a historical work but contains a great deal of additional material, such as long descriptions of the hot season, drinking parties and so forth. This background throws some light on the social life of India towards the end of the 13th century. After the death of Balbān, a Turkish 'Slave-King' of Delhi, the succession was disputed. Nāṣir ud-Dīn Bughrā Khān wanted to succeed his father Balbān when the latter's eldest son Muhammad died, but the dying Balbān chose Nāṣir ud-Dīn's son, Mu'izz ud-Dīn Kai-qubād instead. The son of Muḥammad became governor of the Panjāb and Nāsir ud-Dīn Bughrā ruled over Bengal, but decided to wrest the throne from his son. He invaded Oudh and Mu'izz ud-Dīn Kai-qubād marched to repel his attack. The theme of this poem is the quarrel and reconciliation of Nāsir ud-Dīn Bughrā Khān and his son as a result of a meeting which took place in 1289 on the banks of the river Sarjū in Oudh and the events leading up to this. The manuscript was copied in 1515 but the four miniatures were painted about 1600, judging by the large and loosely-tied turbans (Pl.

XXII). The scene shows worshippers in the Congregational Mosque at Delhi engaged in various stages of Muslim prayer. One holds a rosary like ʻAlī in Plate III. A man who is probably a dervish is kneeling in the foreground. The mosque-lamps, gilded in the miniature, hang on a chain around the dome which the poet says is as magnificent as the chain used for the same purpose in the Kaʻbah at Mecca. The poem opens with a long hyperbolical account of Delhi in which the Congregational Mosque and other important buildings are described.

The illustrations in Add. 27257 belong to the same period as those in Add. 7753. This is a copy of the *Shāhnāmeh* of Firdausī containing fifty-five full-page miniatures with figures of a large size typical of the late 16th and early 17th century. These have a certain naïve charm. The incident shown in Plate XXIII is as follows. Iskandar journeys to the Western Sea where there are men who speak no known language. Seeing a hill rising from the water, shining and yellow like the sun, Iskandar wished to approach it but his wise companions dissuaded him from going nearer. Others of Iskandar's party who entered a boat to take a closer view of the island, were drowned when the boat sank beneath them. Iskandar sailed on until he came to a stretch of water with a swampy shore containing reeds as high as trees of which houses could be built. They went on to a pleasant land, smelling of musk, where they bivouacked for the night. Swarms of snakes and scorpions appeared; also boars with long teeth shining like diamonds and a lion larger than a bull. After escaping from these perils, they sailed on to the land of Abyssinia where the inhabitants, black as crows with glittering eyes like lamps, carry bone spears. The ship resembles an Arab dhow such as those which sail in the Persian Gulf and on the Arabian Sea.

The final phase of Persian book illustration is shown by a miniature from the *Maḥbūb ul-qulūb*, a large collection of moral tales and anecdotes by Barkhvurdār ibn Maḥmūd Turkmān Farāhī called Mumtāz, a prose stylist and poet who is known to have lived in the time of Shāh Ḥusain (d. 1722). This collection, also called *Shamseh va Qahqaheh* from the title of one of the stories, was first known as *Maḥfil-ārā* but the original draft was plundered and destroyed by rebellious tribesmen.

The story from which the illustration (Pl. XXIV) is taken is unmercifully long by reason of the author's attempts at fine writing. It abounds with such bombastic clichés as 'The daughter of the Vizier of Kashmir has hastened from the Pavilion of Existence to the Bed-chamber of Oblivion'. King Kishvar-gushā wished to see a trial of strength between his protégé, the Circassian page Fīrūz-bakht, and his faithful servant and minister Nāṣir whom Fīrūz-bakht disliked. On the appointed day Fīrūz-bakht seized Nāṣir round the waist and strained so that blood came from his finger-tips but he could not move Nāṣir one hair's breadth, although he tried almost two hundred wrestling tricks. At length Nāṣir, 'like a flash of lightning on the harvest', gripped Fīrūz-bakht by the wrist and lifted him bodily from the ground like a child. In his alarm, Fīrūz-bakht held on to one of the pillars of the hall and clung to it with all his might. Nāṣir exerted so much power that the pillar came away. He then threw Fīrūz-bakht and the pillar on the ground with such force that the end of the pillar pierced the brain of Fīrūz-bakht and killed him. The ceiling collapsed and killed two hundred of the spectators. The king and all his court fled in terror. The festival mood became changed to mourning. The costume of the wrestlers (blue drawers with a white design) is still worn in some of the Persian gymnasia (*zūrkhāneh*) where the ancient athletic exercises are practised. Or. 1370, with an elaborate lacquered binding, dates from the year 1800.

# Notes

The transliteration is that used in the British Museum for Persian and Arabic with some slight variations. All letters are pronounced except for the silent 'v' in the combination 'khv'; and 'h' in final 'eh' which is like French 'é'; the vowels marked with a macron are long. The gutturals kh, gh and q are like 'ch' in 'loch', Dutch 'g' and 'k' in 'stuck' respectively. In modern Persian, however, the last two have an identical pronunciation. The ' (e.g. in Sa'dī), a strong guttural in Arabic, is a simple glottal stop in Persian. Other letters are pronounced as in English. The accent is on the last syllable as in French.

1. The following description owes much to Mr. B. W. Robinson's *Persian Paintings* (Victoria and Albert Museum, Large Picture Book No. 6, H.M.S.O., 1952). For the various styles see the detailed and scholarly account by the same author in his *Descriptive Catalogue of the Persian Paintings in the Bodleian Library* (Oxford, 1958).

2. According to the Russian scholar Berthel's, the Muslim equivalent of this date appears on the tombstone of Niẓāmī.

3. The ancient Chorasmia, a land to the west of the lower Oxus.

4. The *Maṣnavī* of Rūmī begins 'Listen to the reed how it tells a tale, complaining of separations. Saying 'Ever since I was parted from the reed-bed, my lament hath caused man and woman to moan. I want a bosom, torn with severance that I may unfold (to such a one) the pain of love-desire. Everyone who is left far from his source wishes back the time when he was united with it.' (Nicholson's translation: with acknowledgments to the Gibb Trustees.)

5. For Qiyat, the family of Chingiz Khān, a subdivision of the Borjigin clan.

6. 'Alī is often called the 'Lion of God'.

7. Nūshīrvān, a contraction of Anūshak-rūbān 'of immortal soul', was a title of Khusrau I (reigned A.D. 531–578).

8. He became as-Saffāḥ (reigned 750–4), the first caliph of the Abbasid line which was descended from the Prophet's uncle.

9. The homily delivered in the mosque on Friday in which intercessory prayer is offered on behalf of the ruler of the state.

10. A subterranean aqueduct, also called *kārīz*.

11. According to Sa'īd Nafīsī, he died in 1230.

12. The Peacock plotted with the Serpent and the Devil to tempt Adam. He was exiled and punished for his part in this by being deprived of his beautiful voice with which he used to sing the praises of God. The Peacock is a symbol of cupidity and man's desire for worldly life.

# Dates

*Dates and Dynasties in Persian History since the beginning of the Christian Era.*

| | |
|---|---|
| Parthians (Arsacids) | B.C. 248–A.D. 226 |
| Sassanians | A.D. 226–642 |
| The Arab Conquest | 636–642 |
| Umayyad Caliphs (Damascus) | 661–750 |
| Abbasid Caliphs (Baghdad) | 750–1258 |
| Sāmānids (Bukhara) | 874–999 |
| Buwaihids (a Shī'ah dynasty) | 932–1056 |
| Ghaznavids (a dynasty of Turkish stock ruling from Ghazneh which is now in Afghanistan) | 962–1186 |
| Seljuk Turks (Great Seljuks and Seljuks of Rūm) | 1037–1300 |
| Khvārazmshāhs | 1077–1220 |
| The Mongol Īlkhāns | 1258–1336 |
| Jalā'irs (Iraq) | 1336–1411 |
| Muzaffarids (Fārs and Kirmān) | 1313–1393 |
| Karts (Herat) | 1245–1389 |
| Sarbadārs (Khurāsān) | 1337–1381 |
| Timurids (the descendants of Tīmūr, better known as Tamerlane) | 1369–1500 |
| Qara-Qoyunlu (Black Sheep Turkomans) | 1378–1469 |
| Aq-Qoyunlu (White Sheep Turkomans) | 1378–1502 |
| Safavids (a Shī'ah dynasty which originated in Azerbaijan) | 1502–1736 |
| The Afghan Conquest | 1722–1729 |
| Afshārs (a Turkoman house founded by Nādir Shāh) | 1736–1796 |
| Zands (reigned from Shiraz) | 1750–1794 |
| Qājārs (another Turkoman dynasty) | 1779–1926 |
| Pahlavīs | 1926– |

# Suggested reading

D. Barrett. *Persian Painting of the Fourteenth Century.* (Faber and Faber Ltd., 1955.)

Basil Gray. *Persian Painting.* (Editions d'Art Albert Skira, Lausanne, 1961.) *Persian Miniatures from Ancient Manuscripts.* (Fontana Unesco Art Books, 1962.)

R. H. Pinder-Wilson. *Persian Painting of the Fifteenth Century.* (Faber and Faber Ltd., 1958.)

B. W. Robinson. *Persian Miniatures.* (Bruno Cassirer, Oxford, 1957.)

B. W. Robinson. *Persian miniature painting from collections in the British Isles* (Victoria and Albert Museum, Large Picture Books, No. 33, London, 1967.)

All these works contain fine colour plates.

A. J. Arberry. *Classical Persian Literature.* (A valuable and readable account of Islamic Persian literature from the earliest times to the end of the 15th century.) (Allen and Unwin Ltd., 1958.)

R. Levy. *Persian Literature.* An introduction. (Oxford, 1945.)

# Index


'Abd ur-Razzāq: 19
Aḥmad i Tabrīzī: 14
*'Ajā'ib ul-makhlūqāt*: 12, 21
Amīr Khusrau: 11, 12, 26
Āqā Mīrak: 22
'Aṣṣār: 17
'Aṭṭār: 10, 14, 20
'Aufī: 12, 16

*Bahmannāmeh*: 14
Barkhvurdār ibn Maḥmūd Turkmān Farāhī: 27
Bihzād: 15, 19, 25
*Būstān*: 11

Daqīqī: 8

Firdausī: 8, 9, 14, 23, 27
Futūḥī: 14

*Garshāspnāmeh*: 14
*Gulistān*: 11, 25

Ḥāfiẓ: 11, 12
*Haft aurang*: 12
*Haft paikar*: 9, 19
Hilālī: 23
*Humāy and Humāyūn*: 11, 13

*Iqbālnāmeh*: 9
*Iskandarnāmeh*: 9

Jalāl ud-Dīn Rūmī: 10, 21
Jāmī: 12, 24
*Javāmi' ul-ḥikāyāt*: 12, 16
Junābādī, Mīrzā Muḥammad Qāsim: 22
Junaid: 13

*Kamālnāmeh*: 11, 13
*Khamseh*: 9, 11, 14, 15, 19, 22
*Khiradnāmeh i Iskandarī*: 12
Khvājū Kirmānī: 11, 13
*Kūshnāmeh*: 14

*Lailā u Majnūn*: 9
*Lubāb ul-albāb*: 16

*Mafātīḥ ul-qulūb*: 11
*Maḥbūb ul-qulūb*: 27
*Maḥfil-ārā*: 27
*Makhzan ul-asrār*: 9, 13
*Manṭiq uṭ-ṭair*: 14, 20
*Masnavī i ma'navī*: 10, 21, 22
*Miftāḥ ul-fuẓalā*: 12, 20
*Mihr u Mushtarī*: 17
Mīrak: 19
Mīr Sayyid 'Alī: 22
Mīrzā 'Alī: 22
Muḥammad Zamān: 22
Mumtāz. *See* Barkhvurdār ibn Maḥmūd Turkmān Farāhī
Muẓaffar 'Alī: 22

*Naurūz u Gul*: 11
Niẓāmī: 9, 11, 12, 13, 14, 15, 19, 22

Qāsim 'Alī: 19
Qāsimī. *See* Junābādī, Mīrzā Muḥammad Qāsim
Qazvīnī: 12, 21
*Qirān us-Sa'dain*: 26

*Rauẓat ul-anvār*: 11, 13

Sa'dī: 11, 25, 26
*Salāmān and Absāl*: 12

Sanā'ī:' 10
Shādīyābādī, Muḥammad ibn Dā'ūd ibn Muḥammad ibn Maḥmūd: 20
*Shahanshāhnāmeh*: 14
Shāh Maḥmūd Nīshāpūrī: 22
*Shāhnāmeh* : 8, 9, 14, 18, 23, 27
*Shāhnāmeh i Ismā'īl*: 22, 23
*Shāh u Gadā*: 23
*Shamseh va Qahqaheh*: 27
*Sharafnāmeh*: 9
Sharaf ud-Dīn 'Alī Yazdī: 24
*Ṣifāt ul-'Āshiqīn*: 23
*Silsilat uz-zahab*: 12
*Subḥat ul-abrār*: 12
Sulṭān Muḥammad: 22
Sulṭān Muḥammad Nūr: 23

*Tuḥfat ul-aḥrār*: 12

'Umar Khayyām: 11

*Yūsuf u Zulaikhā*: 12, 24

*Ẓafarnāmeh*: 24, 25

VII. YŪSUF U ZULAIKHĀ. Or. 4535, f. 104a. The ladies of Egypt overcome by Yūsuf's beauty. Safavid (Qazvin style).

VIII. ẒAFARNĀMEII. Or. 1359, f. 413a. The captured Ottoman Sulṭān, Bāyezīd I, brought before Tīmūr. Safavid (Shiraz style).

IX. JAVĀMI' UL-ḤIKĀYĀT. Or. 11676, f. 113a (*top*). The people swearing allegiance to Abū'l-'Abbās in the mosque at Kūfah. f. 237a (*bottom*). The Caliph al-Mahdī being massaged by his slaves. Timurid (Provincial Shiraz style).

X. MIHR U MUSHTARĪ. Add. 6619, f. 117b. Mihr and King Kaivān playing polo.
Timurid (Southern Provincial style).

XI. SHĀHNĀMEH. Add. 18188, f. 281a. Bahman attempts to kill Rustam by rolling a large boulder on him. Timurid (Turkman style).

XII. MANṬIQ UṬ-ṬAIR. Add. 7735, f. 30a. The dialogue between the Peacock and the Hoopoe. Timurid (Later Herat style).

XIII. MIFTĀḤ UL-FUẒALĀ. Or. 3299, f. 119a. Illustrations to the entries in the glossary for (*a*) a handmill (*right*), (*b*) a standard and f. 286a (*c*) the preparation of a talisman. Timurid (a version of the Turkman style, probably by a Persian artist working in India).

XIV. 'AJĀ'IB UL-MAKHLŪQĀT. Or. 12220, f. 62b (*top*) Iskandar sailing through unknown seas. f. 224b. (*bottom*) a giraffe.

XV. MAS̱NAVĪ. Add. 27263, f. 134a. The elephant attacks the travellers who have eaten her calf. Safavid (Tabriz style).

XVI. KHAMSEH. Or. 2265, f. 203b. Bahrām Gūr killing the dragon. By Muḥammad Zamān. Safavid (Western influence).

XVII. SHĀHNĀMEH I ISMĀ'ĪL. Add. 7784, f. 46b. Shāh Ismā'īl in battle with the Shīrvān-shāh. Safavid (Tabriz style, somewhat provincial).

XVIII. SHĀHNĀMEH I ISMĀʻĪL. Add. 7784, f. 85a. Shāh Ismāʻīl hunting. Safavid (Tabriz style, somewhat provincial).

XIX. ṢIFĀT UL-ʿĀSHIQĪN. Or. 4124, f. 54a. Zulaikhā destroying the idol. Safavid (Tabriz style).

XX. SA'DĪ. KULLIYĀT. Add. 24944, f. 164b. The devotee's camel, on hearing the beautiful singing, throws its rider. Safavid (Shiraz style).

XXI. SA'DĪ. KULLIYĀT Add. 24944, f. 356a. Men bathing in a pool renowned for its healing virtues which is near the tomb of Sa'dī. Safavid (Shiraz style).

XXII. QIRĀN US-SA'DAIN. Add. 7753, f. 17b. Scene inside the Congregational Mosque of Delhi. Safavid (Isfahan style).